Conversations that Matter

Insights &
Distinctions

Landmark Essays Volume 2

Conversations that Matter

Insights &
Distinctions

Landmark Essays Volume 2

Gale LeGassick   Balvinder Sodhi
Steve Zaffron   Jane Wright
Laurel Scheaf   Mark Spirtos
Larry Pearson   Manal Maurice
Cathy Elliott   Barry Grieder

Introduced by Nancy Zapolski, Ph.D. and Joe DiMaggio, M.D.

To Landmark graduates everywhere.

Table of Contents

Introduction

When something moves us, transforms us, makes us feel and think in a new way, it might be considered a measure of greatness. Landmark and its programs have that kind of greatness. Landmark's technology is designed to provide a shift in perspective, an expanded view of what's possible and available to us in being human. This shift is achieved, in part, by presenting a tapestry of linguistic distinctions and terminology that enriches and transforms the way we inquire into *the nature of being human.* These conversations allow for greater access to dimensions of ourselves, and our engagement with others, that we may not have fully explored before.

This second volume by our colleagues, a collection of articles that first appeared in Landmark's quarterly newsletter, explores some of the tenets and principles underlying Landmark's technology. It points out what is possible if we step outside of what we know, and recognize and embrace our capacity to bring forth an entirely new possibility for living—not because it is better, but simply because that is what human beings can do.

These essays are not a written version of Landmark's programs, which are living and breathing events that occur in community and cannot be put into writing. Rather, the essays point to some of the *distinctions* and *inquiries* addressed in that program in a way that is uniquely powerful and transformative.

–Nancy Zapolski, Ph.D.

Joe DiMaggio, M.D.

Coauthors, *Landmark Essays, Volume 1*

Landmark Essay 1

What's "Real?" Is It Open for Invention?

Gale LeGassick

*(Oh, those silly humans! So desperate for their absolutes!)
Sometimes it seems like the only job of the world is to gently (or not so gently) separate us from our deepest assurances... Maybe you, too, were once absolutely sure that you'd found your great love, the perfect financial advisor, or the perfect mentor, meditation, or medication that would—once and for all—never fail you. And then? Slowly, things became not so sure, after all. Such is our slippery toehold on "what's real," and so it has always been.*[1]

Economic fluctuations are a timely (and interesting) lens for examining our toehold on "what's real." Reading the many financial journalists who refer to tales of boom and bust, triumph and disaster, bubbles that inflate and riches that vanish when pins come along to pop them, leads us to question what we once may have thought of as real. How did the money (the multi-millions in hedge funds, stocks, retirement accounts, mutual funds, etc.), if it was really there, just disappear? Was it only blips on a computer screen that existed in our minds in a virtual economy? Comedian Stephen Colbert coined the term "truthiness"—not, he explained, the truth, the whole truth, and nothing but the truth, but rather the truth we *want* to exist."

Or take the world of technology—every day there's new research that requires us to reevaluate fundamental aspects of our existence. Our identities are being pushed, nudged, and twisted by the arrival of new technologies: artificial intelligence, genetic engineering, brain-computer interfaces, biological augmentation, quantum weirdness, etc., challenging our notions of what it means to be human. There is no ironclad definition for some of the terms we most care about, such as life, mind, intelligence, and consciousness. Where do we begin, where do we end? How far could we evolve and still call ourselves human?[2] What's "real"?

When we are born, along with it come multiple lenses, our gene pool, the culture we grew up in, our family environment, all of which go into making up our sense of reality. If we had been born in another time and place, to different parents who had different values, things would be different. When our "realities" and what we've "come to know" get called into question, and the rug pulled from beneath us, we lean toward what's familiar. As much-quoted economist John Maynard Keynes put it: We "fall back on *conventions*, which give us the assurance that we are doing the right thing. Chief among these are the assumptions that the future will be like the past and that the current way things are going correctly sum up future prospects." In other words, we tend to see things that confirm our views more vividly than those that contradict them. However, in attempting to provide coherence, and make sense of things, we often deceive ourselves.

So, in a manner of speaking, we engage in "validity testing" to confirm and back up our sense of things. How we feel, or what we think, for example, like, "I've got a bad *feeling* about this," "I *feel* it's the right move to make," "I *think* his/her expressions of love are sincere." "I *think* you do or don't like me," etc. While we somewhere know our personal thoughts and feelings aren't the most valid tests for determining reality, we use them anyway. We also use tests of *agreement*. We might *agree* that a red traffic light means we should stop, or that a rose is beautiful and garbage is not. A medical authority might say carbs are good or carbs are bad, and because he or she is an authority, that creates agreement that they know what they're talking about. If somebody at work says we look sick, we think it carries less weight than a doctor saying so. We train ourselves to think the more "authorities" say something is so, the more believable that something likely is.

Logic and past experience also factor in here. If we say "pigs can fly," it doesn't sound particularly logical, or reasonable. But saying "pigs run fast" might fit into our logic structure. It used to be illogical and unbelievable that somebody could beat the 4-minute mile or fly to the moon, but when those things happened, we expanded our worldview to include them, and that became a new *agreed-upon* reality. Or we think things are real because materials, physics, laws and other fundamentals (physicalness and measurability) make them so. A chair, for example, is 3 feet high, hard, made of plastic. The family cat, 13 pounds, happily claims the bottom corner of the bed. Or more abstract ideas—like medicine, love, climate change, or government—whether we sit in them, consume them, vote on them, often have a *reality* that we live with and bump up against in our day-to-day lives.

We construct *realities* and then forget we were the ones who constructed them. Our most basic orientation to life is hard-wired, like height or shoe-size. However, a huge percentage of the stuff we are certain about is often wrong—and we have no power with it, and it's hard to see a possibility outside of it. A great line from the movie *The Matrix* says it all: "Welcome to the desert of the real." When our relationship with reality has a kind of "*is*-ness" or "*fixed*-ness" to it, and it's "all that we know," we are at the effect of it—it limits what's possible and allows only for options like explaining, trying to fix, resisting, or accepting. The answer to the question, *what does it mean to be human*, gets looked at only through that lens.

The good news is that "reality" is a phenomenon that arises in language. There is no "is reality"—it's interpretation all the way down. It is all *what's happening* in language. That is all we know and all that we have access to. When we know that words can constrain and enlarge the world—a *word shaping world* becomes a very real thing. As contemporary philosopher Richard Rorty said, "The world is out there, but descriptions of the world are not. The world does not speak. Only we do." Knowing that allows us to shake up those realities we had taken for granted—our own identity, or what we understand words to mean. The shift does not get rid of the lens or filters or mindsets per se, but those filters and mindsets stop defining who we are. With the unsettling of old realities, stepping to one side and another, we become interested in what *might be*, what we can *imagine*, and new worlds, new possibilities open up to us.

This is about creating—and literally bringing into existence—possibilities for living that didn't exist before. Imagination and creativity inhabit the province of possibility. I remember when my stepson, Josh, wrote a poem, I think for his fourth or fifth grade class, and the teacher corrected it. He came home that day asking, "Mom, how can someone correct a poem that you created? It's like correcting a dream." There's a great passage, specific to the world of literature, that further makes this point: "Unlike the multiplication tables or the principles of auto mechanics, imagination and creativity can't be transmitted from teacher to student. Imagine Milton enrolling in a graduate program for help with *Paradise Lost*, or Kafka enduring the seminar in which his classmates inform him that, frankly, they just don't believe the part about the guy waking up one morning to find he's a giant bug."[3] Possibility does not engage things in a clear-cut way (black/white, good/bad, true/false). Things that live as a possibility in our lives have a much different impact on the quality of our lives than those things that live as just "the way it is." Creating possibility is basically how we get to know what's possible in being human. This is what it's all about.

Landmark
Essay 2

The Underpinnings
of Breakthrough
Performance

STEVE ZAFFRON

Every company in every industry works under certain forces or laws that influence what that company can and can't do. The ancients who attempted to fly by strapping feathered wings to their arms and flapping with all their might as they leapt from high places invariably failed. Despite their dreams and hard work, they were fighting against powerful forces of nature. Flight became possible only after they came to understand the relevant laws.[1]

Just as understanding the relevant laws of gravity, physics, or probability theory make certain things possible—flight, building bridges, financial windfalls—there are laws that apply to the art and science of performance. In our recent book, *The Three Laws of Performance*, Dave Logan and I identify laws that address the underpinnings of effectiveness, achievement, and breakthrough results, both in business and our day-to-day lives.

This story from Philip Roth seems apropos: "Suppose you and I went up to the ballpark together, and there's a guy next to us with his kid. And he was saying to his kid, 'Now, what I want you to do is watch the scoreboard. Stop watching the field. Just watch what happens when the numbers change on the scoreboard. Isn't that great? Now, do you see what just happened up there? Did you see what happened? Why did that happen?' And you say, 'That guy is crazy.' But the kid imbibes it and he goes home and he's asked, 'How was the game?' And he says, 'Great! The scoreboard changed thirty-two times and Daddy said last game it changed only fourteen times and the home team last time changed more times than the other team. It was really great! We had hot dogs and we stood up at one point to stretch and we went home.'

"Is that politicizing the game? Is that theorizing the game? No, it's having not the foggiest idea in the world what [the game] is."

We have much the same fogginess about what actually causes breakthrough performance, or causes anything for that matter. Most of what we're familiar with about what causes what we've learned from a

14

"cause and effect" model. Causality is a very solid, respected, and useful way of looking at the world. It has produced an enormous amount of valuable information, in terms of what shapes outcomes and behavior. However, if we are aware that causality is just one model for understanding the world and that it is sometimes but not always useful, we are more likely to use it when it works, and not when it doesn't.

There's another model that's also powerful in terms of shaping outcomes and behavior. This model has the additional dimension and advantage of giving us access to the very source of performance. We call this the "correlate" model, and it brings us to the first law of performance we address in the book: Performance is not always caused by or an effect of something, but rather is correlated to—or in a dance with—the way the world shows up for us. To say it again, performance is a result of how the world (or a situation, or a circumstance, or a person) occurs for us.

From time to time in Vanto Group's consulting engagements, I'll bring along a tennis ball and ask someone who considers themselves unathletic or uncoordinated to help demonstrate this first law. I say to the person, "I'll throw the ball; you catch it and return it to me." I toss the ball and the person attempts to catch it, but they pretty much fumble each time. Then after a few throws I say, "We're now going to change the game—it's no longer catching the ball, the new game is to call out which way the ball is spinning as it comes toward you." For the first two or three throws, the person doesn't catch the ball when I toss it. He or she calls out which way it's spinning accurately, but the ball just lands on the floor—and they go after it, pick it up, and lob it back. After a couple of throws, the person begins naturally catching the ball, as well as calling out which way it was spinning—not even aware, really, that the ball is being caught time after time.

In both versions of the game, the person's performance is correlated to how the world occurs for him or her. In the first part, behavior was correlated with the thinking of being uncoordinated, in the second, to being competent or able. Performance in both situations is related to one thing only—how the world occurs for a particular person.

The second law of performance has to do with the role of language. Oversimplified, the perspectives of "catch this ball, which we already know we can't catch" and "calling out which way the ball is spinning, which we know we can do quite well" (same ball, same speed) lead to two totally different outcomes. Each perspective is constituted in language—it is in language that we articulate, define, and shape reality. It is the conversation in each game that yields completely different performance outcomes.

We carry such conversations around with us about how things are—how we or our corporations measure up, what's possible and what isn't, how things work, what we know to be true. When we say that things are a particular way, we become constrained and limited to what that reality allows—it's just "the way it is." To coin a phrase, it becomes an "is world," and an "is world" has a particular design to it—it's solid, fixed, and we have to adjust to it. We spend much of our lives struggling with "the way things are," rather than savoring the malleability that a constitutive view of language can lend to our world. How things occur—occurring—is a linguistically based phenomenon. Language is integral to accessing breakthrough performance. But as posed in the first law, our actions are not correlated to an "is," fixed, or static world; rather they are correlated to an "occurring" world.

The third law of performance has to do with future-based language. When we know it is our conversations that constitute our world, it shifts our relationship to what's possible. It puts us in the driver's seat. The shift doesn't necessarily get rid of the lens or filters or mindsets per se, but fixed notions, old assumptions, old realities stop defining what's possible and what's not. We most commonly use and think of language in an experiential, descriptive, or representational way—as a response to the world, a process of fitting or matching our words to the world as we know it. Let's call it a word-to-world fit. This use of language allows for certain outcomes, but not others. In a future-based model, language is used in a generative or contextual way, and is more than a response to the world. It yields completely different outcomes and is actually what brings the world into being–a world-to-word fit. In this model, language is both what gives rise to the world and what gives access to what is in that world.

With that premise, we say that reality, conditions, and circumstances of the future do not exist as facts, but rather as a product of our conversations. Assuming that's the case gives us a certain dominion, a direct and powerful access to shaping performance, to shaping outcomes. This generative, future-based model dynamically and actively pulls for the fulfillment of whatever future we are out to create.

Take Akio Morita, former chairman and cofounder of Sony, who said he would change what "Made in Japan" means. He wasn't just interested in his company's performance or a particular product line, but a shift in thought globally as well as in his own country. "Made in Japan" at that time was associated with cheap, poor-quality items. He redefined the phrase to embody leading-edge technology, quality, and the highest levels of customer satisfaction on a worldwide scale. He also created new futures for Sony's products; he spoke of listening to songs while walking about at a time when nobody believed in the marketability of a tape player that couldn't record–the Walkman was the result. History is strewn with examples. Louis Pasteur set out to demonstrate that microscopic organisms caused disease and propelled medicine into a new era; the writers of the Magna Carta (by establishing the principle of limited government) altered the world stage for human rights; Kennedy's declaration made manned space exploration a reality.

There's something very important in these examples– each represents a future not existing at the time. There's a certain declarative or generative language that was used in each case and the game unfolded in a new direction based on what a person or group of people said. A declaration made by an individual or group isn't him or her or them speaking "about" something, but is the thing itself–it's language that actually creates something, brings something forth–the declaring into existence an intention, a stand, something with an impact, a space of possibility.

Possibility is not real at its origin–it's something we create as real, and then stand for as a reality. And when possibilities such as those mentioned above are created and articulated as a future, the terrain of the present occurs differently for people. Future-based language, in other words, contains the direction and momentum in which and for which things move. It folds the future back into the present, and when that happens people's actions become correlated to that future and their performance alters in the present. These three laws are about rewriting the future now, and also knowing we have the wherewithal to do that ongoingly.

Landmark Essay 3

Power and Possibility—Inventing a New Kind of Time

LAUREL SCHEAF

When it comes to the nature of time, physicists for the most part are at as much of a loss as the rest of us, who seem hopelessly swept along in its current. The mystery of time is connected with some of the thorniest questions in physics, as well as in philosophy, like why we remember the past but not the future, how causality works, why you can't stir cream out of your coffee or put perfume back in a bottle.[1] The central metaphor in Stephen Jay Gould's entertaining book, Wonderful Life: The Burgess Shale and the Nature of History, *is that the history of life can be thought of as a video tape. One can imagine rewinding life, and by some*

23

divine miracle, changing a pivotal scene at the beginning, and then rerunning life again from that point. If we turned out the lights, flipped the cassette at random, and then played it, would a visitor from another universe be able to tell if the tape was running properly forward or unconventionally backward?[2]

And who's to say what's "properly forward" or "unconventionally backward"? We, and almost all cultures in the world are shaped by the notion of a past, a present, and a future. The main presumption of existence is that life is one thing after another. Time, whether marked by the tick of the clock or the majestic expansion of the universe, so permeates our senses, so defines memory and expectation, that it is elusive by its ubiquity. One can't even be sure whether time is an abstraction, or as real as rocks. But one thing seems clear to the average person: Time is a one-way, no return, take-your-lumps deal. Hence the mild surprise with the question whether time has to go one way and not the other, and whether the universe could not run backward perfectly well...[3]

Past, present, and future, is a conceptual way of speaking about time and being. Our existence is a past, present, and future kind of existence, yet, past, present, and future aren't immutable facts. But before we go further, consider how our current notions of time actually play out. Instead of three kinds of time, it's more the case that it really splits into two: a past/present and a present/future kind of time. We are never really in the present—mostly it's as if we're floating between the past and the future. We are localized in the present, yes, but our overlay—our relationship to the present—is never just the present itself, it's either the past/present or the present/future. Of the two, the pull invariably is for the past/present.

We can see this past/present pull everywhere—especially when we have a particularly good or bad experience. If it's a bad experience, like getting bitten by a dog, let's say, we're prone to be wary of dogs (no matter how much we may subsequently learn about dogs being friendly). If it's a good experience—some great success, receiving a special acknowledgment—we log that into our future, too. We try to remember the steps that got us there, hoping to capture the specifics for future use, or as Tom Robbins amusingly puts it, "we become frozen in that glad ice, turning ourselves into living fossils for the remainder of our existence." Whether our experiences were good or bad, instead of locating what happened in the past, we put those past memories and the decisions we made about them out in front of us—into our future. Our future then becomes shaped, and filtered through those decisions, limiting what's even seen or imagined as possible.

When I was a kid, I owned one of those magic slates. You drew on it with a plastic stylus, and when you'd lift the plastic sheet and all the marks you'd etched would disappear—a clean slate would appear each time.

(Would that it were so easy with our lives.) Since the past is registered and etched and filed into the future, it appears as if it is the past is what determines the present, but it isn't. What actually does have the influence is the future we're living into. It is the future that shapes who we are being in the present. Think about it. What inspires us, and what moves us, or what stops and defeats us, is essentially due to how we see the future in front of us. We don't have much experience, maybe none, at taking the past out of the future. But if the past was taken out of the future—either by putting it back where it belongs, or by virtue of recognizing it for what it is—it would no longer have the impact and influence it once had. We would have a lot more freedom—way more room to move. Or in Robbins' words, "Living fossils [would] begin to unfreeze themselves from the glad [or bad] ice and come back to life."

When the past is no longer calling the shots, the question becomes: "If I weren't my past, who would I be? What would be possible?" The ways we know ourselves, what we can and cannot do, what's possible or impossible, would no longer be a given. Standing in the future, informed but not limited by the past, the possibilities for our lives multiply exponentially. It does not merely change our actions or give us new choices, it gives a completely different quality to life in the present.

Possibility is an element of temporality. Starting from possibility reverses the flow—it becomes a future/present pull. This future/present pull changes the game entirely. Even at its earliest stages, possibility leaves us with power and freedom. Altering the temporality of things is not just a matter of time—it's a matter of the quality of our lives. Kurt Vonnegut said in his last book: "I think one of the biggest mistakes we're making has to do with what time really is. We have all these instruments for slicing it up like a salami, clocks and calendars, and we name the slices as though we own them, and they can never change—'11:00 AM, November 11' for example—when in fact they are as likely to break into pieces or go scampering off as dollops of mercury. Might not it be possible, then, that seemingly incredible geniuses like Bach and Shakespeare and Einstein were not in fact super-human, but simply plagiarists, copying great stuff from the future?"

Landmark
Essay 4

The Freedom of Being: Beyond Right/Wrong, Win/Lose, etc.

LARRY PEARSON

This passage comes from *The New York Times:* "Long before seat belts or common sense were particularly widespread, my family made annual trips to New York in our station wagon. Mom and Dad took the front seat, my infant sister sat in my mother's lap and my brother and I had the back all to ourselves. We'd lounge around doing puzzles, reading comics, and counting license plates. Eventually we'd fight. When our fight had finally escalated to the point of tears, our mother would turn around to chastise us, and my brother and I would start to plead our cases. 'But he

31

hit me first,' one of us would say, to which the other would inevitably add, 'But he hit me harder.'

"It turns out that my brother and I were not alone in believing that these two claims can get a puncher off the hook. In virtually every human society, 'He hit me first' provides an acceptable rationale for doing that which is otherwise forbidden. It is thought that a punch thrown second is legally and morally different than a punch thrown first. The problem with the principle of *even-numberedness* is that people count differently. People think of their own actions as the consequences of what came before, they think of other people's actions as the causes of what came later, and that their reasons and pains are more palpable, more obvious and real, than that of others."[1]

The stuff of wars, soap operas, divorce courts, Hamlet, and more all borrow on that equation, as do we. While we might wish we'd left that *even-numberedness* to our childhood and adolescence, it's not to be. The dynamic of dealing with issues that are unwanted, yet persist continues to play out in board rooms, neighborhoods, marriages, and between nations—we justify, we blame, we complain.

Issues that are unwanted, yet persist can be a powerful impetus for change, as evidenced by the progress of human rights, for example. But there's another world of things that are unwanted, yet persist—things that we complain about over and over, like some aspect of our relationships or jobs that is not working, and yet we find ourselves keeping around.

If we put what's "unwanted, yet persists" together with "fixed ways of being," we get what we call a "racket." It's a "mashup" of sorts (a web buzzword). In a mashup, one web application is combined with another, making both applications more productive and robust—you get something greater than the sum of the parts. If you mash up what's unwanted, yet persists (which is most likely occurring as a complaint) and a *fixed way of being,* you also get something greater than the sum of its parts, but in this case, the yield heads in the wrong direction—the combination is unproductive or more accurately, counterproductive.

A *complaint* is some kind of opinion or judgment of the way things "should" or "shouldn't be." The evaluative component isn't a commentary on facts that are true or false, accurate or not, but again how we think things *should* be. By *fixed way of being* we mean acting in a predictable and repetitive manner (like always frustrated, always upset, always angry, always nice, always annoyed, always suspicious, always confused, etc.). Whatever our *fixed way of being* is, it's not something we have a choice over. It's just there—it shows up automatically when the complaint shows up. It's also worth noting that a recurring complaint doesn't *cause* the way

33

of being, nor does the way of being *cause* the recurring complaint—they simply come together in one package. The whole point here, though, is that it's a *fixed way of being*, not a *possible way of being.*

The term "racket" comes from the days of big-city gangsters and street-level criminals who conducted questionable activities—loan-sharking, bribery, larceny—usually set up to get some kind of payoff, camouflaged by an acceptable cover above suspicion. In a "racketeering" operation, the efforts at concealing what's going on behind the scenes can become quite elaborate so as to protect and ensure the success of the operation. We borrow the term *racket* as it's applicable to our contemporary lives and because it carries with it many of the same properties—deception, smoke screens, payoffs, etc.

Sometimes persistent complaints originate with us, other times they come *at* us from someone else. It's harder to see that we're in "racket mode" with complaints that come *at* us, because it looks like somebody *else* is the persistent complainer, and we just an innocent bystander. But under closer scrutiny, it turns out we too have complaints—complaints about their complaints. Our matching complaint might show up like, "don't they understand, don't they know how it is for me, why are they nagging, don't they see everything I'm doing for them?" When we complain, we feel quite justified that our response is appropriate to the situation.

We explain the rationale behind our complaints to interested (and uninterested) parties, and point out how pleased we are with ourselves for taking the necessary steps to sort things out—we have a certain fondness for our *attempts*, for "trying." We might get our friends, family, or coworkers to agree that we're dealing with our complaints the best we can. If they point out that perhaps we're the one perpetuating the problem, we could feel misunderstood, put out, even busted. Seen from a distance, there can be something almost endearing about how we go about all this—as if it's part of our authentic and sincere spirit—but actually, our rationale for doing what we do is another thing entirely. This is the camouflage or cover-up part. The deceptive nature of a racket and the allure of the payoff keep us from realizing the full impact rackets have in our lives.

The payoffs for keeping rackets around usually show up in several ways: being right and making others wrong (not the factual kind of right, but thinking that we *are* right and the other person is wrong), being dominating or avoiding domination, justifying ourselves and invalidating others (attributing cause to some thing or person other than ourselves), engaging in the win/lose dynamic (not "winning" like a celebration with trophies, applause, or congratulations to the opponent, but winning such that someone else is the loser or is lessened in some way). These payoffs are like facets of a diamond—although one facet might be more dominant than another (and we might deny or not be aware that some aspect of a payoff is active in our case), they're really all at play.

The pull of these payoffs is often compelling enough to get us to give up love, vitality, self-expression, health, and happiness. That's a ridiculously strong force. Those costs are the standard fare of a racket. It's pretty obvious that we can't be happy, vital, and loving while we're making someone wrong, dominating someone, being right, or justifying ourselves—one displaces the other. This is where choice comes into the picture.

Rackets, although one thing, have two forms of existence (somewhat like ice and steam are two forms of H_2O). One form of a racket shows up as "I *am* X, Y, or Z." The second shows up as "ahhh, I *have* a racket that is X, Y, or Z." When we *are* the racket, it shapes and determines our way of being. But when we *have* a racket, it has very little power over our way of being. We have a choice about what's at play—about giving up our rackets, our positions, our unproductive ways of being. When we elect to transform our default ways of being—being right, coming out on top (the even-numberedness, so to speak)—we move to a place of freedom, a place of possibility. The question then becomes: How do I express my life? What would be, for me, the most extraordinary, created, invented life? It becomes a matter of art, of design. How extraordinary are the everyday aspects of our lives; how rich our lives are, how full of opportunity, when we act on the possibility of living life fully.

Landmark
Essay 5

Relationships: Alive with Possibility

CATHY ELLIOTT

Harper's Magazine published a piece by Laura Kipnis called "The Domestic Gulag." The author offers a brief sample of answers to the simple question: "What can't you do because you're in a couple?" (This information, she points out, is all absolutely true; nothing was invented. Nothing needed to be.)

You can't leave the house without saying where you're going. You can't not say what time you'll return. You can't go out when the other person feels like staying home. You can't go out just to go out, because you can't not be considerate of the other person's worries about where you are, or their natural

41

insecurities that you're not where you should be, or about where you could be instead. You can't leave your (pick one) books, tissues, shoes, makeup, mail, work, sewing stuff . . . lying around the house. . . . You can't amass more knickknacks than the other person finds tolerable—likewise sports paraphernalia. You can't leave the dishes for later, wash the dishes badly, not use soap, drink straight from the container, make crumbs without wiping them up (now, not later), or load the dishwasher according to the method that seems most sensible to you. . . . You can't talk on the phone when they're in the room without them commenting on the conversation, or trying to talk to you at the same time. You can't read without them starting to talk, and you're not allowed to read when they're talking to you. You can't use the "wrong tone of voice," and you can't deny the wrong-tone-of-voice accusation when it's made. . . . You can't ask for help and then criticize the mode of help, or reject it. . . . You can't express inappropriate irony about something the other person takes seriously. . . . You can't not be supportive, even when the mate does something insupportable. . . . You may not criticize the other person's driving, signaling, or lane-changing habits. etc., etc., etc.

Lots of our behavior in relationships is driven by complaint. How powerful are a person's actions when those actions are the product of complaint? It's doubtful we know any truly powerful people whose actions are shaped and driven by complaint. Complaint weakens our actions and our thoughts and our feelings. "The possibilities that exist between two people, or among a group of people, are a kind of alchemy. They are the most interesting thing in life," says contemporary poet, Adrienne Rich. She goes on, in essence, to say, "When relationships are driven by complaint or by keeping track of who did what, or the need to be right, to control, they likely possess a dreary, bickering kind of drama, but cease to be interesting. The wonderful world of human possibilities ceases to reverberate through them."

At some point in our relationships with our partners, our coworkers, family members, it seems we have the thought that we're not fully satisfied. Even if there are long stretches where things are great, at some juncture we find ourselves disappointed about something, or feel that something is missing–that our particular relationship(s) are not all we'd hoped for. And once those thoughts make their way to consciousness, a refrain is sure to follow. Dissatisfaction invariably follows satisfaction, because what we so often do with satisfaction is try to hold on to it. Satisfaction held on to, however, becomes mechanical–the antithesis of satisfaction. In William Blake's words, "He who binds to himself a joy/Does the winged life destroy." Satisfaction can't be held on to like a thing, it can only be created. To create something requires a space in which to create, and when that space isn't there, most likely it's because we're holding on to something incomplete from the past.

Completing things comes down to a matter of getting beyond the "yeah buts" and "how 'bouts" and the "but ifs," "onlys," and "whens" about how things "should" or "need" to look a particular way. Completing things frees us up. It doesn't automatically imply that everything is going to be just dandy in the future, but it does mean that we can address whatever there is to address in our present-day relationships, instead of dramatizing whatever might have been incomplete from the past. When something is complete it is *as it is*, there is not a need for something else. It's *as it is* without being obscured by the way it *should be*. The *should-bes, ought-to-bes*, the way we *want it to be*–our ideals or comparisons with other things, other people, other times–all kind of drop away. There isn't a sense that things "must" be different. It might be pleasant or preferable to have things be other than they are, but there isn't an attachment to having something else, or a need for some part of it not to be there. The point is that something can be *missing like a possibility* vs. "missing" *as if it is wrong or bad*. When something's missing as a *possibility*, there's not a sense of insufficiency or inadequacy–there's an allowing for and an acceptance of *the way it is*. What's missing here doesn't exist like a *thing*, but rather as a *possibility for something*–and with that comes a freedom.

Each of us has experienced moments in our lives when we are fully alive–when we have no wish for it to be different, better, or more. We have no disappointment, no comparison with ideals, no sense that it is not what we worked for. We feel no protective or defensive urge—have no desire to hold on, to store up, to save. Such moments are perfect in themselves. We experience them as being complete, and know a space within ourselves where such moments can be generated. It's a shift or a state change, from being a character in a story to being the *space* in which the stories occurs—the author, as it were, consciously, freely. It is a transformation—a contextual shift from the content in our lives being organized around *getting* satisfied—to an experience of *being* satisfied.

And because relationships exist in language (not just as a set of feelings or accumulation of experiences, for example), there's a malleability, a plasticity, a can-be moved-around-ness about them. When we walk around dissatisfied, thinking the other person *should* be different in one way or another, or say something like "they never really understood us," or that "their expectations were unwarranted," or "their idiosyncrasies were annoying," what is really happening is that we are saying that. And the other person is likely *saying,* in some manner or another, what's so for them. In all cases, it's people *speaking* to themselves, *speaking* to others, or other people *speaking* about other people *speaking* to each other—it's all occurring in language. When we shift

45

the locus of our dissatisfaction and complaints from something "out there" to which language can only *refer*, to something that is located "in" language, what's possible shifts.

It's not necessarily a fact that we'll be satisfied if such-and-such happens in a relationship, or doesn't happen. Being satisfied is not a feeling later labeled with the word "satisfaction"; rather it is a commitment, a stand we're taking for that possibility. That stand becomes the "chute" down which what we're "up to" can be realized. When that happens, the conditions and circumstances for our relationships begin to reorder and realign themselves. How we see and hear others and how they see and hear us is transformed. This is what it's all about–to be satisfied *before* anything happens.

Landmark
Essay 6

Revealing Our Selves to Ourselves

BALVINDER SODHI

Heat was a profound puzzle in the early 19th century. Every-one intuitively knew that a hot object cooled to its surroundings and a cool object likewise warmed up. But a comprehensive theory of how heat really worked eluded scientists, as it had to explain some weird happenings. Hot things expanded; cold things contracted. Motion could disappear into heat. Heat could spark motion. When certain metals were heated, they gained weight, therefore, heat had weight. Early explorers into heat had no idea that they were investigating temperature, calories, friction, work efficiency, energy, and entropy—all terms they were to invent later.[1]

And so it is today with explorers who are attempting to come to grips with the elusive self-conscious "I"—to provide some insight into just what exactly goes into the nature of being human. From fields of philosophy, brain science, anthropology, linguistics, psychology, etc., people are actively investigating, inventing, and picking through strands of disparate evidence. For most of us, "I" is positional ("you" are there and "I" am here), a location in time and space, a point of view that accumulates all previous experiences and points of view. Does this "I" presume a substantial entity located inside our bodies, or is it located in our minds, our families, job titles, Facebook profiles, bank accounts—those trappings that help us maintain the meanings and understandings that we have up 'til now *considered ourselves to be?*

Theories abound. Sherlock Holmes was said to sometimes look for the logic of human behavior in plumes of pipe smoke; Shakespeare thought people became themselves through action and dialogue; Darwin saw human activity related to that of apes, albeit slightly more clever; Freud attributed the development of self to a cauldron of drives and motives of which we are largely unconscious. The Bhagavad Gita attributed human behavior to our attachments to our false or temporal selves in our material world. Philosophers Heidegger, Sartre, and Husserl thought the self's way of existing to be a function of their involvement in worldly activities–physical, social, and historical. Biologists have tipped their hats to the genetic code (a matter of molecules); brain scientists to neural activity.

While theories and explanations are useful, also of enormous value is having direct, hands-on access to *who we are* as human beings–to being able to actually impact our actions, to change course should we so desire, to be the authors of our own lives. The single biggest stop to having this kind of access is one of *identity* (the "who" it is that we consider ourselves to be), coupled with the impulse we have to cling to and defend whatever notion of ourselves we already have. How we "arrive" at our identity is mostly inadvertent– essentially built from a series of what we see (consciously or not) as failures to *do* or *be* something. When these "apparent" failures arise, we make decisions about how to compensate for, respond to, and accommodate ourselves to them. So whether it is one or 10 or even 40 years later, when something inconsistent with how we see ourselves occurs, we still hold on to that with which we've identified–leaving us no powerful *way to be* with whatever is going on.

The degree to which our behavior is filtered by our identity goes unrecognized–the *default* filters then set our values; bestow meaning; determine the aims, limitations, and purpose of our daily life. They become "us," they are "us," and we only get what they allow—obscuring access to ourselves and to what's really possible in being human. Unless the *identity* factor is addressed, the answer to the question, *what does it mean to be human*, gets looked at only through that lens. But stepping outside of our identity isn't so easy—as it's achieved a certain density throughout our lives—it is all we know of ourselves. The idea that another whole idea of *self* is available can be disconcerting, invalidating. In setting aside "all the usual things that gave us an 'identity'—the accident of our time and place of birth, the accident of being a human being rather than a dog or a fish—we become aware that this so-called *self* is as arbitrary as our name. It's like standing over an abyss, recognizing that 'I,' as we know it is not an absolute."[2] But it is here, with this recognition, where transformation occurs.

Transformation does not merely change our actions, it uncovers the structures of *being* and interpretation on which we are grounded. This revealing of our selves to ourselves occurs in a profound way that can alter the very possibility of what it means to be human. And while transformation is not an event, there is a definite before/after quality to it. Transformative learning gives us an awareness of the basic structures within which we know, think, and act in the world. This shift does not rid us of old contexts, it simply stops defining who we are. That is the single most powerful attribute of Landmark's work.

"I am" is the language of identity. "I occur," on the other hand, kind of jolts that perspective, orientation, and notion of ourselves. Each moment's meaning happens inside of the background of understanding against which it occurs. The phenomenon of *occurring* begins to reveal and dismantle what we might normally have attributed to a "cause-and-effect" model or a just "the way things are" model of thought. But we don't act out of what is there or what we know, or a cause-and-effect model—we act out of what "occurs"—our actions are directly correlated to how the world *occurs* for us.

For example, if the world "occurs" to us that it's important to win, we take a lot of risks (we can't win if we don't); if the world occurs for us that it is important to avoid losing, we take very few risks (as we can only lose by taking risks). How the world occurs gives two totally different kinds of lives. Renowned physicist Richard Feynman wrote that two mathematically *equivalent* formulations can "occur" *unequal.* People investing their money who are told they're likely to lose money every 30 years, invest differently than if they're told they have a 3.3% chance of losing a certain amount each year.[3] Same math, but occurring differently.

Another great example of this, as we sometimes demonstrate in our programs, is when we ask somebody who considers themselves very uncoordinated to play a game of catch. We throw them the ball, and as expected, they don't catch it. When we change the game and ask them to just call out which way it's spinning, they think of themselves as fully able to make the call accurately, and at the same time they (inadvertently) catch each ball. Changing the game alters the way it "occurs" for the player.

In each of these examples, what people are *saying* to themselves (how the world "occurs" for them) results in two totally different outcomes. *Occurring* is a phenomenon that arises in language. Language is much more than just a vehicle for describing or representing reality. To access the power of language–beyond words themselves–calls for a transformation from knowing ourselves as our identities (that is, *who we have considered ourselves to be*), to knowing ourselves through language. We shift in the way we define ourselves–not merely in the way we think about our definition of self, nor merely in the way we believe our self to be, but in the actual experience of who we are as the one who *defines* who we are. *Who we are* is fundamentally a conversation–a phenomenon of language, created by our words–by our saying.

When identity stops being something that is fixed, real, or just the way it is, there is this ability to generate possibility. It's worth seeing the difference in what an *identity gives* versus what *possibility gives.* Identity gives a "condition" in which life occurs. Possibility is a "clearing" in which life occurs. Possibilities are generated; conditions are by default. When we recognize that we are not our identities, and the space of nothing becomes available, *who we are* can show up as itself. It is from nothing that we have the space in which to create. From nothing, we can create something we know we created, so we don't get stuck with what we create, because we can again create something else. Transformation leaves us with the presence of choice—no more, no less. The actual choosing remains of our own making.

Landmark
Essay 7

Trumping the Vicious Circle, Changing the Game

JANE WRIGHT

Historically, there was something like a Trojan war, maybe even several Trojan wars in fact, but the one Homer wrote about in the eighth century B.C. is the one that fascinates us, because it is fiction. Archaeologists and historians doubt that any Trojan war began because someone named Paris kidnapped someone named Helen from under the nose of her Greek husband, or that it was a big wooden horse filled with soldiers that finally won the day. You can find no trace of them in the diggings in northwest Turkey in what might have been the real Troy. But who would give up the Iliad for the historical record? Legends, myths, dreams—all of it is grist for

59

the mill. Nothing is excluded, certainly not history. Historians and fiction writers alike decide what is relevant to their enterprise and what isn't. Some facts are brought to light, others left in darkness. History undergoes a constant process of revision. Reality is amenable to any construction placed upon it.[1]

Like historians and novelists, we too construe our own histories as *we* see them—and realities get created accordingly. Here's how it works: Something happens. We simultaneously assess and interpret what happened— assign meaning, categorize importance, draw conclusions, identify action to be taken (or not), form opinions that linger. This melding or collapse between *what happens* and *the meaning we assign to it* happens so instantaneously that we somehow lose all memory that *what happened* and *how we hold it* were two independent and separate occurrences.

Consider there are two domains of distinction, two ontological domains in our day-to-day living: one in which life shows up as an *experience,* and another in which life shows up as a *representation* of, or a *concept* about that experience. We essentially live in the collapse between the two. Our experience invariably devolves into a representation of the experience—memories, concepts, and descriptions of life (which are not life, but descriptions of it). We then experience subsequent events through these *already* existing conceptual frameworks. A conceptually-shaped *experience* reinforces the *concept* that shaped it. The reinforced *concept* more fully shapes the *experience*. The more fully shaped experience reinforces the concept some more and it goes round-and-round like this. Thus its name: the *vicious circle*.

Another way of saying it is: When something happens and we make whatever assessments we make at the time, we believe and think them valid. We think our conclusions are epiphanies of sorts–kind of indisputable, bottom-line truths. We see reality and ourselves in terms of that truth–as if it were us, not something separate or outside of us. We also map our behavior and future experiences onto it. Our identity, our persona, who we are, and how we see ourselves gets reinforced again and again–a "vicious circle" indeed, because of its relentless and mechanical nature. What's disempowering in this *vicious circle* thing is not the interpretation or meaning we immediately assign, but rather the *collapsing* of those interpretations with *whatever it is that happened*. It is in the collapse that realities get set.

Those "realities" become the stuff and story of our lives. We can spice up or water down our stories, tell the long or short version, add drama or subtlety. Regardless of how clever we are, or what new or different set of circumstances we put into the *vicious circle*, what we get out of it is only what is gotten out of a vicious circle—varied, yes, but it is essentially *more of the same.* While we might think our stories new and unique, it inevitably turns out that there are only two or three basic themes playing themselves out over and over, often in ingenious ways.

Now, there's nothing actually wrong with stories. In fact, I love the richness, the tapestry, the depth of our stories—the moments we savor, the experiences we share, really are the stuff of our lives. If we think for a moment about those most precious people in our lives, each of them has a special story that's uniquely their own—how we met our spouses, a time when a friend's kindness made a difference, something we heard or saw that was so hilarious we nearly cried. It's hard to imagine a life without the intricacies and intimacies of those moments—it would be a bit dull and boring.

Our stories represent the richness of what it means to be human—there is a power and validity, a value in them, but not when they're confused with the presence of life. (Being in the *presence* of something is, obviously, quite different than being in the *concept* of it.) Which brings us to what we might call the downside of stories—the side where our interpretations keep us stuck, where we get into the vicious circle.

When we begin to see inside the mechanical nature of this *vicious circle*, its bankruptcy becomes apparent. It would be great if the slate were clean and we could be determining the principles by which we were going to fill the slate, but in a *vicious circle* no intentionality, and no created purpose can exist. *Vicious circles* are formed in reaction to something– mechanically, not intentionally.

When we ask ourselves the question, "Does my life matter, do I make a difference," the only possible answer in the vicious circle is "I doubt it." It's not that we can't or don't make a difference, it's just that in that particular circularity or the swirl, if you will, of the vicious circle, there is no space for anything to make a difference. And when we become aware of the bankruptcy, we would more than likely go about attempting to change it–but "change" only alters the circumstances in the same circle. While there's no *fixing it* in the vicious circle, in the recognition of it being at play we can begin to "uncollapse" the two worlds and see ourselves separate from it. By recognizing the bankruptcy, we have a say in the matter of *who we are*, and the room to create and design our lives.

Knowing our stories are an interpretation (no more true or false than another interpretation), and that that's not *who we are*, produces an opening, an access, a portal to a third domain–the domain of being. Possibility exists in the domain of *being* and isn't available in the other two domains. It is here, in this domain, that we are able to create something from nothing–an existential act, and one that can hold both the experience and the circumstances. Possibility moves things around until our experience and our circumstances are a match for the possibility we've created. Distinguishing that is transformational. It shifts the horizon of what's possible.

Landmark Essay 8

Navigating Our Lives:
What Really Matters

A particularly avid sailor shared with me a piece he'd
read about celestial navigation: "...you begin by *pre-
tending* you know exactly where you are—with fiction.
On a chart you mark your position, a dark point on
blank water. You call this your *ded reckoning* position.
The *ded* comes from *deduced,* what you think you know
based on history: the history of the boat, how fast she
has been moving, and in what direction. You draw a
line along your true course: five hours, say, at 6 knots
equals 30 nautical miles of distance along that course
line from your last known position, the place where
you think you are now. This is what you believe. Up
until this moment, it has been the basis for all your

decisions regarding the voyage, yet you are [if need be] willing to abandon it.

"[To check your calculations] you open your navigator's tool kit—star finder, compass, chronometer, parallel rules, triangular protractor, pencil, stopwatch, etc. And you prove yourself wrong: you're not where you thought—and if you're a good navigator, hopefully, not too far from where you thought you were. In proving yourself wrong, you prove something else: exactly where you are. It is not a matter of opinion, not open for debate, not arguable or biased by gender or ethnicity or influenced by national regimes or political agendas, not personal. You either miss the reef or you hit it. You either find the sea buoy that marks the entrance to your harbor or you pass it by. You make landfall or you don't. That's the beauty of navigation. It is unequivocal."[1]

A lot of things in our day-to-day lives have a malleability to them, a flexibility. Multiple options are available—we can go one way or another, and whatever our choice, things can turn out OK. With celestial navigation, however, that's not the case, nor is it the case with integrity. Both have this built-in unequivocality to them. While it's easy to appreciate the consequences of being a few degrees off course when at sea, it's not as immediately obvious in the matter of integrity.

The notion of integrity has intrigued us for a long, long time. It never stops being relevant–whether we hear about it in monarchies, politics, financial practices, scientific research, or ancient mythology. Thousands of books are written on the subject, millions of web searches take place. Integrity was ranked as the most looked-up word on the web at one point. The notion of integrity usually comes with a lot of associations– there's something that the word already means or doesn't mean to us, some reaction or point of view we have about it. Many people think of integrity as synonymous with morality–being ethical, a good person, an upstanding citizen, or doing the right thing. Each understanding has a certain validity and an important and central place in personal, professional, and societal life. Yet the potential power of each word (integrity, morality, ethics, goodness) can be lessened when meanings are collapsed and mushed together with other meanings. *Integrity* is actually a phenomenon in and of itself–one that goes beyond what we might mean by morality or ethics. It's one that has more to do with *authenticity*–being true to ourselves–and it is the foundation for power and effectiveness.

"Integrity" comes from the word *integer*, meaning "whole, complete, and missing no component or part." If we think about a computer chip or a bicycle wheel, for example, and if in the making of it some small part was left out, neither would be able to function as they were intended. Any disruption in the integrity of something's design, however small, impacts its workability and function. When something is whole and complete, it is not good per se, it just works. The same holds true for the "being" part of being human. When the wholeness and completeness of *who we are* is jeopardized in some way, however small, that begins to alter our life, even if at first it's imperceptible or unnoticeable.

It's in those moments when we might say to ourselves, "it's just a one-time thing," or "no one will ever know," that we unwittingly alter our baseline of integrity and compromise who we are. We might experience a sense of discomfort or unease, or if we're justifying ourselves, we might spend time defending, explaining, or pointing fingers. When our integrity is out in some way, we find ourselves tolerating a level of unworkability, and because it's usually gradual and occurs in small increments, we never seem to fully come to grips with how much impact it has on things not working in our lives. A baseline that was once at 100% is now 99 or 98 or 70%–and while most people don't notice it, the difference between 99 and 100% is *everything–* it is in that 1% that the quality of our life alters. So when our baseline for integrity moves to 98 or 97 or 70%, our sense of ourselves becomes more and more obscured, making it harder and harder over time to return to who we are.

Resignation and cynicism begin to show up—not so much in the obvious or expected ways, but more so in things like being reasonable, acting negatively, being upset. There's a certain momentum that builds. The most subtle form it shows up in might be such comments as "While things may not be great, they are as good as they can be." We convince ourselves that we're not free—that our actions are determined by our circumstances, our natures, whatever. But freedom isn't dictated by circumstances. Our actions are only determined by our free, unconstrained choices. In being true to ourselves, being authentic and honoring our word, we tip the scales. Integrity and living a life of power and effectiveness are inseparable. Instead of the *already/always condition* setting the limits on *who we are*—our *saying* becomes the gravitational pull for *who we are*. When we live our lives consistent with our word, when we experience ourselves as whole and complete, we create the possibility of freedom and power.

We face, every moment, the choice of who to be and what to do. As with celestial navigation, integrity is not a place to arrive, but what we use to steer the ship—integrity is unequivocal. Integrity is a matter of choice, and the matter of choice is uniquely human.

Landmark Essay 9

Myth Busting—Context Is the Game Changer

MANAL MAURICE

There's an old story that is basically true: Ordinary Roman carts were constructed to match the width of ruts in the road that the war chariots had left. The chariots were sized to accommodate the width of two large horses. Roads throughout the vast Roman empire were all built to this spec. When Romans marched into Britain, roads were constructed at that width. When the English started building tramways and railways, the width stayed the same. British laborers built railways in the Americas using the dimensions they were accustomed to.

Fast forward to the space shuttle. The two large solid fuel rocket engines on the side of the launch shuttle were sent by railroad, and to be transported were designed to be the same width. A major design feature of what is arguably the world's most advanced transportation system was determined over two thousand years ago by the width of two horses. More or less, this is an example of how knowledge can create constraints, gain momentum, and over time harden and become nearly unchangeable.[1]

Much of what we "know" we know because someone else told us it was so. Knowledge that's handed down, inherited, is in one sense, "everybody else's," yet we often end up living within its parameters. We filter what we see through a somewhat distorting lens of past experience, language, tradition. Information that has the force of history or science behind it (or just the force of habit), but doesn't fit with our existing frameworks, has a hard time being seen, heard, accepted. Add to that the notion that those frameworks have correlated frames, which further skew our view of things. What we reject and what we accept, in retrospect, often seems a bit odd. Something keeps us in these little areas of what we *already know*—we call it the three-part myth of "is, because, and I."

1. The first component of the myth is the notion of "is," which implies that there is a "fixed" world out there with an existence independent of us (giving us the perspective of spectator vs.

player in the game). We often take for granted that things *are* a particular way, solid, fixed, something we have to adjust to. We become constrained and limited to what that reality allows—it's just "the way it is."

2. "Because" is the second component. This one can keep us caught up in a "cause and effect" model (and thinking that's the only model). However, our actions are not always caused by something, or an effect of something, rather they are correlated to—or in a dance with—the specific way the world shows up for us. Recognizing that takes us completely out of the cause-and-effect world and gives us an access to ourselves that is unavailable in the cause-and-effect loop.

3. Lastly, there is the component of "I," which refers to the *who it is we consider ourselves to be* (that we can get stuck with, because we mistake that for *who we are*). *Who we consider ourselves to be* is essentially arrived at by default. We put together these ways of being from a series of decisions and reactions (appropriate, perhaps, at one time)—but essentially built from a series of what we see (consciously or not) as failures to *do* or *be* something.

When our relationship with the world lives inside this three-part myth, we are left only with the "after-the-fact" realm of description, analysis, explanation—in other words, *at-effect.* Our options are only to fix, resist, change, etc., and we have no access to the full panoply available to us in being human—no power, no access to breakthroughs.

Before we can dismantle this myth, we have to recognize that it's operative. If we stop and look (at how we're being, what we're saying, etc.), we can see that we're coming from a particular place—one that keeps giving us the set of outcomes we have. For example, if someone tells us something's possible, and we say "we already tried that, and it wasn't possible," our framework is likely that whatever it is "doesn't work, and isn't going to work," and all that that implies. Seeing our operative frameworks is a bit like seeing the backs of our eyeballs. And when we do see them, we can shift them. When Einstein realized, for example, that matter and energy, time and space were not separate entities, but all aspects of a whole, everything was transformed. Old knowledge took on new meaning. Breakthroughs happen not because of startling new facts, but because of a change in the overall way that the universe is seen. They require going beyond the figurable, beyond the reasonable, beyond the domain in which we "know."

Szymborska, a poet and Nobel laureate, said, "Whatever possibility is, it's born from a continuous 'I don't know.' This is why I value that little phrase so highly. It's small, but it flies on mighty wings. It expands our lives to include the spaces within us as well as those outer expanses. If Isaac Newton had never said to himself 'I don't know,' the apples in his little orchard might have dropped to the ground like hailstones and at best he would have stooped to pick them up and gobble them with gusto. Had Madame Marie Curie never said to herself 'I don't know,' she probably would have wound up teaching chemistry at some high school."

How we hold things—our contexts, our frameworks—sets the values, limitations, and direction of our daily lives. They impose on the external world our version of reality. It can take a long time to shift our contexts—whether they're personal or those involving our relationships, our established traditions, or the culture of an enterprise—not because it takes a long time to bring about change, but because we go about it at the level of "content." In dealing with the content, we are extending the existing world rather than creating a new possibility in the world. We can't muck around with context with the same set of equipment we use to deal with content. When things aren't working or we want a breakthrough, it's the "context," not the content, that's the game changer.

Dealing at a contextual level puts us entirely at another level of effectiveness and creativity, and requires a different set of tools. We have something to say about the contexts we come from. When we function at a level of context, old frames stop defining who we are. It's not that we escape them—it is rather that we escape thinking automatically, reflexively. Once we've made the distinction between *how we see things* and *who we are, what we see* becomes a function of who we are. Nothing is more exciting than to see the world in a new way, because we don't see one new thing— we see everything in a new way. The previously unimaginable becomes possible.

Landmark Essay 10

Breakdowns: A Catalyst for Breakthroughs

BARRY GRIEDER

Create a possibility, a commitment, a goal, put it out in the world, and its inevitable brethren—breakdowns *and* the idea that there shouldn't be any—arrive right along with it. Breakdowns are a fact of life, and come packaged in a particular way: even though we know they're inevitable (something we're *clear* is going to happen at some point), we're also surprised when they come up because we think they *shouldn't be* happening in the first place. That particular dynamic causes upsets. Add in the *reactions* we have to it happening, and voila, the domino effect gets set in motion.

Breakdowns (whether over life's unexpected setbacks, missed opportunities, love affairs gone bad) often carry with them some association with, or hint of, failure. When we set out to do or be something and our plans are thwarted or something "goes wrong," there's a disparity between *what happened* and *what the possibility was.* But instead of sorting out whatever happened, we often relate to the disparity as a statement about *us*– some shortcoming, some deficiency. Our *identity, who we consider ourselves to be,* jumps to front and center. Refrains like "What's *wrong* with me?" "What's *wrong* with it?" "What's *wrong* with the ubiquitous 'them'?" are the litanies we hear in our heads. In the answers to those questions, though, there aren't any facts, or truths per se–there are only interpretations, judgments, and assessments. When we operate on top of disempowering assessments (of ourselves, others, particular situations), our ability to *be* gets diminished.

A perfect example is when I started doing triathlons. I'd always considered myself athletic, fast, could keep up with the best of them, etc. I started training, ramping up every week, and when the day of the triathlon came, I considered myself fit and ready. I saw myself crossing the finish line if not in the first 10%, at least in the top 20%. What happened, however, was a whole different matter–at some point, I realized I was going to finish maybe in the last 40%. The steep hills, the

84

distance swimming, the miles in front of me never seemed to end. It was a bit embarrassing for me to see how far off I was, and I quickly fell into that old "what was I thinking?" refrain. It was one of those moments when you don't know what to be in a dance with—the conversation in your head or the possibility. My disappointment actually had me question whether I'd continue doing triathlons, but what was worse was that this line of thinking began extending out to other areas of my life, insidiously shaping what I thought was possible. In retrospect, this was ridiculous, but there it was.

It's this compounding effect (the breakdown *about* a breakdown, the upset about an upset) that is the problem, not that some *thing* in particular went wrong. Another way of saying it is, it's the "failing to be" that takes us off course, not that "it failed." When our commitment to creating something gets thwarted in some way, we can get frustrated, lower our expectations, accommodate, become resigned. As long as we keep identifying with our feelings and the circumstances, thinking that when things go wrong it is a statement about us, we pretty much preclude having a different outcome.

The notion of failure, as we all know, comes with baggage, and it's hard to dislodge those associations. We think failure implies there's a deficiency at some level, that the outcomes we're after won't be achieved, or that they will be jeopardized in some way. For the sake of this piece, let's say that a *failure* is different or distinct from a *breakdown*. (In actuality though, both are assessments, interpretations, and only exist as a phenomenon of language.) But given there's less baggage associated with the word "breakdown" (and because of that, more malleability), using that word offers a different clearing or space to address breakdowns effectively. So let's just say for the moment that breakdowns (given they live in language) are a *making up*, an *invention*. They are a *declaration of something missing*, not necessarily followed by a "therefore" or a "because," but just existing as themselves.

Breakdowns and upsets and disappointments–they're not going away. But what we can do is leave behind old conversations like: "circumstances are a way *because...*" and its corollary "I am powerless *because...*" Intentionally listening for "what's missing" might at first seem difficult, because it has that invalidating ring to it. But if instead of seeing *what's missing* like it's "too bad," we can see it as a possibility, it can fundamentally alter the game. Instead of a "failure of being," what's there is the possibility of "inventing being." Breakdowns as an *invention*, as a *saying*, as a *making up*, afford us a larger opening–power and freedom have room to emerge.

When we are up to something, and step outside the constraints of our circumstances, and stand for a possibility that we don't know how to achieve, we don't reference what's possible against who we'd been or what had been done in the past, what's predictable or expected, but rather against what we stand for and saw is possible. While this might sound simple, the transformative impact of seeing breakdowns this way is also enormously far-reaching. In my triathlon example, the transformative quality extended into my professional life, being a dad, having a fantastic relationship with my wife—far beyond the possibility of that one circumstance.

When we see this, life begins to be seen and related to differently. Our relationship to possibility moves from an abstract ideal to a viable, living reality—we find ourselves taking bold, practical action that gives what we stand for the hard edge of making something happen.

When the possibility of power begins to arise, it can get a bit scary. What if things go wrong? What if they work brilliantly? An almost automatic, built-in lock on "no power" comes into play. I remember reading that within a few months of Václav Havel's ascension as president of Czechoslovakia, when the euphoria of the Velvet Revolution began to fade, Havel said that he felt "strangely paralyzed." "At the very deepest core of this feeling there was, ultimately, a sensation of the absurd: what Sisyphus might have felt if one fine day his boulder stopped, rested on the hilltop, and failed to roll back down. It was the sensation of a Sisyphus mentally unprepared for the possibility that his efforts might in fact succeed, a Sisyphus whose life had lost its old purpose."[1]

Breakthroughs are usually preceded by uncertainty and breakdowns. If we limit the ambiguity, the floundering about, the experimentation, we limit what's possible and deprive ourselves of the raw stuff from which possibilities arise. Having power, success, and freedom is a lot more risky than having no power. Again, we'll for sure encounter breakdowns on the way, and go through the practice and add the steps in–but we're adding the steps *into* the possibility, not trying to build *towards* the possibility. There is a transcending of the ordinary rules. The ordinary rules are: we learn a little bit, then we learn a little bit more, then more, and finally we know enough. But when standing for and coming from a possibility, life begins to be seen and related to differently. Conditions and circumstances begin to reorder and realign themselves inside of what we stand for. We find ourselves acting in wholly new ways–taking bold, practical action that gives what we stand for the hard edge of making something happen.

Endnotes

ESSAY 1

1. Adapted from Elizabeth Gilbert, "What I Know for Sure About Certainty," *O, The Oprah Magazine*, October 14, 2008.

2. Adapted from Kevin Kelly, "The Technium and the 7th Kingdom of Life," *Edge: The Third Culture*, July 19, 2007.

3. Francine Prose, "Close Reading," *The Atlantic Monthly*, Fiction Issue, 2006.

ESSAY 2

1. Adapted from Clayton M. Christensen, "Introduction," *The Innovator's Dilemma: The Revolutionary Book that Will Change the Way You Do Business*, New York: HarperCollins, 2003.

ESSAY 3

1. Dennis Overbye, "Remembrance of Things Future: The Mystery of Time," *The New York Times*, June 28, 2005.

2. Kevin Kelly, *Out of Control: The New Biology of Machines, Social Systems, and the Economic World*, Cambridge, Mass.: Perseus Books, 1995, p. 408.

3. Charles Petit, "Time Trajectories," *San Francisco Chronicle*, June 30, 1991.

Essay 4

1. Adapted from Daniel Gilbert, "He Who Cast the First Stone Probably Didn't," *The New York Times,* July 24, 2006.

Essay 6

1. Adapted from Kevin Kelly, *Out of Control: The New Biology of Machines, Social Systems, and the Economic World,* Cambridge, Mass.: Perseus Books, 1995, p. 404.

2. Adapted from Colin Wilson, *The Mind Parasites,* Berkeley, Calif.: Oneiric Press, 1990.

3. Adapted from Nassim N. Taleb, Daniel G. Goldstein, and Mark W. Spitznagel, "The Six Mistakes Executives Make in Risk Management," *Harvard Business Review,* October 2009.

Essay 7

1. E.L. Doctorow, "Notes on the History of Fiction," *The Atlantic Monthly,* Fiction Issue, 2006.

Essay 8

1. Adapted from Philip Gerard, "Adventures in Celestial Navigation," pp. 245-252, in Lee Gutkind, Ed., *In Fact: The Best of Creative Nonfiction,* New York: W. W. Norton & Company, 2004.

Essay 9

1. Adapted from Kevin Kelly,"Temporary Becomes Permanent," *Kevin Kelly's Lifestream,* August 13, 2008, and Kevin Kelly, "Chosen, Inevitable, and Contingent," *The Technium,* July 10, 2009.

Essay 10

1. Adapted from David Remnick, "Exit Havel," *The New Yorker,* February 17, 2003.

About the Authors

The authors of this book, Landmark faculty members, conduct leading-edge programs designed to maximize personal and organizational effectiveness. Internationally respected for their forward-thinking ability to deliver provocative new perspectives, these authors come from a great variety of backgrounds—doctors, lawyers, business leaders, philosophers, and scientists.

The programs they lead inquire into the basic structures in which we know, think, and act in the world and are powerful catalysts for change. This collection of essays will transform the way we think about ourselves, our families, our work, our communities—what we're up to in life.

About Landmark

Landmark is a global leader in the field of training and development, offering courses and seminars that are innovative, effective, and immediately relevant. Landmark's programs are designed to bring about a fundamental shift or transformation in what is possible in people's lives.

A fundamental principle of Landmark's work is that people and the communities and organizations with which they are engaged have the possibility of not only success, but also fulfillment and greatness. It is to this possibility that Landmark and its work are committed.

Find out more by visiting
www.landmarkworldwide.com